American Lives

Thomas Jefferson

Rick Burke

Heinemann Library
Chicago, Illinois

© 2003 Heinemann Library
a division of Reed Elsevier Inc.
Chicago, Illinois

Customer Service 888-454-2279

Visit our website at www.heinemannlibrary.com

Created by the publishing team
at Heinemann Library

Designed by Ginkgo Creative, Inc.
Photo Research by Kathryn Creech
Printed and Bound in the United States by
Lake Book Manufacturing, Inc.

07 06 05 04 03
10 9 8 7 6 5 4 3 2 1

Library of Congress Cataloging-in-Publication Data
Burke, Rick, 1957-
  Thomas Jefferson / Rick Burke.
    v. cm. — (American lives)
Includes bibliographical references and index.
Contents: Jefferson — Childhood — Law and Monticello — Marriage and Books —
Talents — The coming war — Declaration of Independence — War years —
Serving Washington — Presidency — Louisiana Purchase — Last years —
Remembering Jefferson.
  ISBN 1-40340-160-8 (lib. bdg.) — ISBN 1-40340-416-X (pbk.)
  1. Jefferson, Thomas, 1743-1826—Juvenile literature. 2.
Presidents—United States—Biography—Juvenile literature. [1.
Jefferson, Thomas, 1743-1826. 2. Presidents.] I. Title.
  E332.79 .B87 2002
  973.4'6'092—dc21
                    2002004144

Acknowledgment
The author and publishers are grateful to the
following for permission to reproduce copyright
material: p. 4 Burstein Collection/Corbis; pp. 5, 11,
12, 19, 21, 25 The Granger Collection, New York;
p. 7 Dave G. Houser/Corbis; p. 8 Lee Snider/
Corbis; p. 9 David Muench/Corbis; p. 10 Photri; p.
13 North Wind Picture Archives; pp. 15, 17, 20R,
23R, 26 Bettmann/Corbis; p. 16 Corbis; p. 18 Scott
T. Smith/Corbis; p. 20L The Corcoran Gallery of
Art/Corbis; p. 22 AP/Wide World Photos/White
House Historical Association; p. 23L Archivo
Iconografico, S.A./Corbis; p. 27 Kit Kittle/Corbis;
p. 28 Charles E. Rotkin/Corbis; p. 29 Jeremy
Woodhouse/PhotoDisc

Cover photograph: Bettmann/Corbis

Special thanks to Patrick Halladay for his help in
the preparation of this book. Rick Burke thanks
John . . . remember I'll always be your big brother.

Some words are shown in bold, **like this.** You can find out what they mean by looking in the glossary.

For more information on the image of Thomas Jefferson that appears on the cover of this book, turn to page 26.

Contents

Jefferson .4

Childhood 6

Law and Monticello 8

Marriage and Books 10

Talents .12

The Coming War 14

Declaration of Independence 16

War Years 18

Serving Washington 20

Presidency 22

Louisiana Purchase 24

Last Years 26

Remembering Jefferson 28

Glossary *30*

More Books to Read *31*

Places to Visit *31*

Index *32*

Jefferson

From 1801 to 1809, Thomas Jefferson was the third president of the United States. He is remembered as a good president, but some things about him seem strange to some people.

Gilbert Stuart, an artist born in Rhode Island, painted this picture of Jefferson in the early 1800s.

For example, he owned slaves throughout his life, but he helped stop the buying and selling of slaves in his home state of Virginia. Jefferson was a wonderful writer whose words are read by schoolchildren all over the world, but he had trouble talking to people in his everyday life.

Jefferson Firsts

- *First **governor** to be elected president.*
- *First president to live in the White House, which was then called the President's House.*
- *First widower to be elected president. A widower is a man whose wife has died.*

Jefferson also was a man who wasn't happy with being good at just one thing. He did many things in his life, including being a lawyer, inventing, raising plants, watching nature, and designing buildings. He wanted to do the best he could in whatever he tried.

People probably remember Jefferson most for writing the **Declaration of Independence,** which declared the United States to be a free nation.

This statue of Jefferson was made by Jean-Antoine Houdon in 1789.

Childhood

Thomas Jefferson was born on April 13, 1743, in Virginia. At the time, Virginia was a **colony** of Great Britain, the most powerful country in the world. Thomas's parents were Peter and Jane Jefferson. Peter was a surveyor, which is a person who measures land and makes maps.

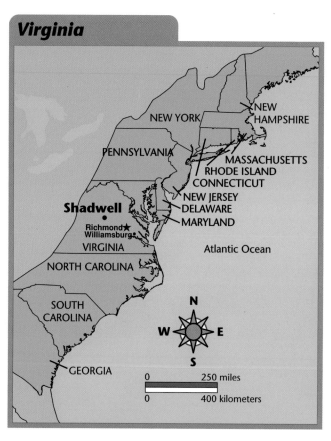

Virginia

NEW YORK
NEW HAMPSHIRE
PENNSYLVANIA
MASSACHUSETTS
RHODE ISLAND
CONNECTICUT
NEW JERSEY
DELAWARE
MARYLAND
Shadwell
Richmond★
Williamsburg
VIRGINIA
Atlantic Ocean
NORTH CAROLINA
SOUTH CAROLINA
GEORGIA

N
W E
S

0   250 miles
0   400 kilometers

Peter made enough money to buy land in Virginia. There, he built a **plantation** called Shadwell, where slaves grew tobacco. The tobacco was sold in Great Britain, and the Jeffersons became a wealthy family.

The Life of Thomas Jefferson

1743	1760–1762	1776	1779
Born on April 13 in Shadwell, Virginia.	*Attended College of William and Mary.*	*Wrote* ***Declaration of Independence.***	*Elected* ***governor*** *of Virginia.*

Students still attend classes at the college Jefferson went to in Virginia, the College of William and Mary.

Young Thomas loved being outdoors. He also loved to read. **Tutors** helped him learn how to read books in the languages of Latin, Greek, and French.

When Thomas was fourteen, his father died. Thomas thought he could help out his family by finishing his education. At sixteen, he entered college in Williamsburg, Virginia. While he was at college, Thomas read fifteen hours a day for weeks at a time.

1789	1796	1801	1826
Became first secretary of state of the U.S.	*Elected vice president of the U.S.*	*Became third president of the U.S.*	*Died on July 4 in Monticello, Virginia.*

Law and Monticello

After college, in 1762, Jefferson decided to become a lawyer. In Jefferson's lifetime, people learned the law by working in a lawyer's office. Jefferson chose to work in Williamsburg with George Wythe, a friend who was a lawyer.

Williamsburg

*Williamsburg was the center of Virginia's government. The British **governor** who was in charge of running Virginia lived there.*

Jefferson spent five years learning his new job. He wanted to know how each law began, how it was important, and how laws were alike and different in other countries.

Visitors to Williamsburg are able to see what the town looked like in Jefferson's time.

Workers started building Monticello in 1769, using Jefferson's first design. In all, there are 43 rooms in the building.

In about 1767, Jefferson began designing a house for himself. His neighbors built their homes in a valley, but Jefferson had a different idea. He had his house built on a mountain peak in Virginia. It looked down on the Piedmont Valley and had a view of the Blue Ridge Mountains.

He named his home Monticello, which means "little mountain" in Italian. Jefferson spent more than 40 years designing and redesigning the home. It still stands today.

Marriage and Books

In 1770, his parents' **plantation,** Shadwell, burned to the ground. Jefferson's mother and sisters came to live with him at Monticello, which was just a small building at the time.

The fire destroyed Jefferson's book collection. Jefferson started collecting books again, and three years after the fire, he had collected 1,250 books. When he died, he had more than 6,500 books. He

The U.S. government's Library of Congress has a building named for Jefferson, seen at the top of the photo above.

wanted to learn as much as he possibly could.

Jefferson's Books

In 1814, British soldiers burned the United States government's official library, the Library of Congress. Jefferson offered his book collection to replace the burned books. In 1815, the government paid Jefferson almost $24,000 for 6,487 books.

There are no paintings of Jefferson's wife. This is a picture of their daughter, Martha, who was born in 1772.

Jefferson fell in love when he met Martha Wayles Skelton. She liked the same things that he did. She danced and read books. They also loved to play music together.

They were married on New Year's Day in 1772 at her father's house, which was 100 miles (161 kilometers) away from Monticello. The couple had to travel back to Monticello during a bad snowstorm.

Talents

Jefferson had many talents. He made money as a lawyer, but he also invented things that are still used today.

Jefferson invented the swivel chair, a chair in which you can spin all the way around in your seat. He also invented the dumbwaiter. A dumbwaiter is like a small elevator inside a wall that is used to bring plates, food, and drinks from one floor to another.

Jefferson invented this writing desk. It was built in about 1775. He used it to write wherever he wanted to, even outside.

In Jefferson's time, rice was grown in fields like this one.

Jefferson was also proud to be a farmer. He wanted America to be known as a nation of farmers. He brought plants from around the world to the **colonies.** He used the plants to make American crops better.

Jefferson thought American rice could taste better. He brought rice from the country of Italy back to America after he took a trip there. He used this rice to create better rice in America.

Jefferson the Scientist

Jefferson used a telescope to map planets, stars, and comets. He also kept a journal of the daily weather.

The Coming War

In 1765, **Parliament** in Great Britain put a tax, or an extra charge, on newspapers and other printed things. The **colonists** argued against the tax. They found that by working together, they could get things done more quickly and easily. In 1766, Parliament stopped the tax.

In 1767, Parliament made the colonists angry again. The colonists had to pay taxes on tea, paper, ink, and glass. The colonists thought that their own **legislatures** should control how people lived in the colonies.

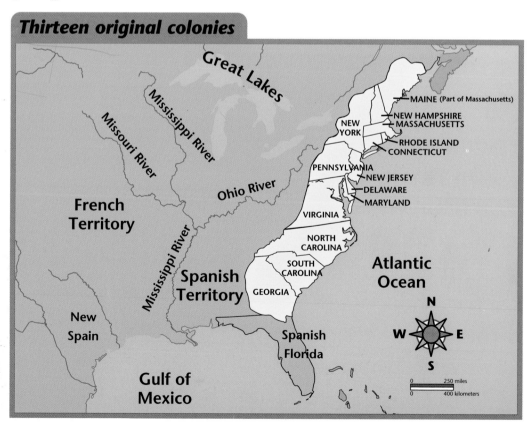

Thirteen original colonies

Great Lakes

Mississippi River

Missouri River

Ohio River

MAINE (Part of Massachusetts)

NEW HAMPSHIRE
MASSACHUSETTS

NEW YORK

RHODE ISLAND
CONNECTICUT

PENNSYLVANIA

NEW JERSEY

DELAWARE

MARYLAND

VIRGINIA

NORTH CAROLINA

SOUTH CAROLINA

GEORGIA

French Territory

Spanish Territory

New Spain

Mississippi River

Spanish Florida

Atlantic Ocean

N

W

E

S

Gulf of Mexico

0   250 miles
0   400 kilometers

The colonists started a **boycott.** Most colonists refused to buy anything taxed by Parliament. The boycott hurt the British because they were not making any money.

The boycott worked. Parliament stopped the tax on everything but tea. In 1773, a group of men in Boston, Massachusetts, thought the tea tax should be ended, too. On the night of December 16, the men dressed up like Indians and climbed aboard three British ships. They dumped 342 chests of tea from the ships into the harbor. Today, this night is known as the Boston Tea Party.

Other colonists cheered as the men threw the tea into the water.

Declaration of Independence

The **colonists** continued to be angry with Great Britain's government. They thought it wasn't fair that **Parliament** could tax them if they weren't allowed to vote for their leaders.

Anger about the taxes was one reason the **Revolutionary War** started on April 19, 1775. British and American soldiers fired guns at each other that day in Massachusetts. Soon after, each of the colonies sent respected leaders to Philadelphia, Pennsylvania, to form the Second **Continental Congress.** Jefferson was sent from Virginia. The Congress was formed to find a way to be free from Great Britain's rule and to prepare for the coming war.

This is an early version of the Declaration of Independence, handwritten by Jefferson.

The Congress accepted the Declaration on July 4, 1776, and signed it.

In June 1776, the Congress wanted to have someone write out the reasons America deserved to be free. Because he was such a good writer, the other men picked Jefferson to write the words. About two weeks later, the **Declaration of Independence** was finished.

In beautiful and clear language, Jefferson told the world why the colonies of America should no longer be a part of Great Britain. Jefferson's words showed the world that the colonists would fight to end British rule. It was the birth of the United States of America.

War Years

Jefferson went back to Virginia to serve in the new **legislature.** The legislature's job was to make laws, pass taxes, and lead the **colonists** during the war.

Jefferson believed that if the Americans won the war then the United States could be different from other countries. He didn't want his country to be led by just the rich, like in Great Britain. He wanted farmers and people who didn't own much land to have an equal say in how the government was run.

This statue of Jefferson is in the Jefferson Memorial in Washington, D.C.

Jefferson was very proud of some laws that he helped to write. He wrote laws that helped boys and girls get an education. He also helped with a law that gave everyone in Virginia the freedom of religion. Each person could worship in his or her own way.

In Jefferson's time, children went to school in classrooms like the one in the picture above.

A Family's Land

Jefferson got rid of an earlier law that gave all of a family's land to the oldest son when a father died. Now, the other children in families could share the land.

Jefferson also helped write a law that said no more slaves could be brought into the state of Virginia.

Serving Washington

Jefferson served as Virginia's **governor** from 1779 to 1781. In 1782, his wife, Martha, died after giving birth to Lucy, their sixth child.

In 1784, the United States government asked Jefferson to travel to France to join John Adams and Benjamin Franklin. Their job was to make sure the United States stayed friendly with France's government leaders.

Franklin and Adams worked as a part of a team with Jefferson.

While Jefferson was there, the French people went through a **revolution.** They wanted to start a government like the United States had.

Martha

Martha gave birth to six children during her marriage to Thomas. Only two, Jefferson's daughters Martha and Mary, lived to be adults.

Henry Knox, Alexander Hamilton, Jefferson, and Edmund Randolph were all chosen to help Washington.

The French asked Jefferson to write a constitution. But Jefferson believed that it wasn't right for an American to write the laws of another country.

Jefferson returned from France in 1789 and became President George Washington's secretary of state in 1790. Jefferson's job was to make sure the United States was friendly with other countries.

In 1796, John Adams became president. Jefferson got enough votes in the election to become the vice president. But Adams and Jefferson ended up having very different ideas about how to run the government.

Presidency

Adams and Jefferson had been friends for many years, but they had different ideas about how the president should lead. Their differences made them enemies.

Adams and Alexander Hamilton, another of George Washington's helpers, wanted a strong national government. Jefferson thought that the states should have more power. He believed that giving the states more power would let common people have more say in how the government was run.

This picture of the White House, then called the President's House, was drawn during Jefferson's presidency. It was in a book that came out in 1807.

In 1800, Jefferson and Adams both wanted to be elected president. Hamilton didn't want Adams to be president, so he wrote a booklet that said why. A lot of people read it, and Adams didn't get as many votes as Jefferson.

Hamilton, left, was killed in a gunfight with Burr, right, in 1804. Hamilton had said mean things about Burr at a party.

Jefferson and his partner in the election, Aaron Burr, ended up with the same number of **electoral votes,** a tie! The election had to be decided by another vote in the **House of Representatives.**

Burr had friends in the government that at first stopped Jefferson from getting enough votes to be named president. After 36 rounds of voting, Jefferson was finally named president, and Burr became vice president.

Louisiana Purchase

The United States became much bigger when Jefferson was president. Spain had given most of its land in North America to France. This worried Jefferson because Napoleon Bonaparte ruled France. Jefferson didn't want him to get close to the United States. Jefferson had a helper ask Napoleon if the United States could buy a city that France controlled.

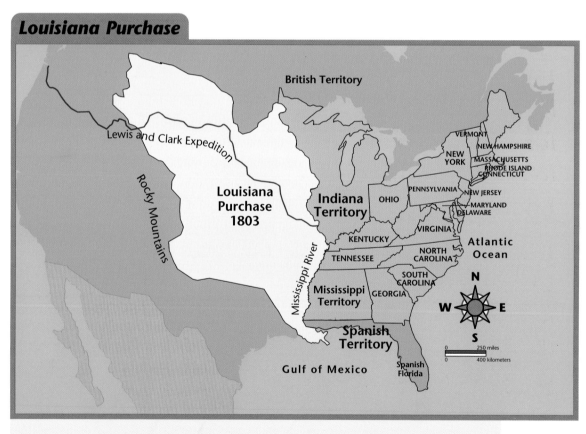

Louisiana Purchase

British Territory

Lewis and Clark Expedition

Rocky Mountains

Louisiana Purchase 1803

Indiana Territory

OHIO

PENNSYLVANIA

VERMONT

NEW HAMPSHIRE

NEW YORK

MASSACHUSETTS

RHODE ISLAND

CONNECTICUT

NEW JERSEY

MARYLAND

DELAWARE

VIRGINIA

KENTUCKY

Atlantic Ocean

Mississippi River

TENNESSEE

NORTH CAROLINA

SOUTH CAROLINA

Mississippi Territory

GEORGIA

Spanish Territory

Gulf of Mexico

Spanish Florida

N
W — E
S

0   250 miles
0   400 kilometers

When Jefferson bought the Louisiana Territory, which stretched from the Mississippi River to the Rocky Mountains, it doubled the size of the country.

An Indian woman named Sacagawea helped Lewis and Clark talk to Indians they met on their travels.

Jefferson was very surprised when Napoleon offered to sell the whole Louisiana Territory for fifteen million dollars. Jefferson agreed to the deal, which is known today as the Louisiana Purchase.

Jefferson sent Meriwether Lewis, William Clark, and about 40 other men to explore the new land. On May 14, 1804, the men began their trip. They were gone for more than two years. They found strange plants and animals and met different Indian tribes. They also mapped lakes and rivers and traveled to places that only Indians had seen before.

Last Years

Jefferson was elected to a second **term** as president in 1804. His next four years in office were not as successful as his first four.

Rembrandt Peale painted this picture of Jefferson in 1805.

Sailors on British ships were capturing American sailors and forcing them to work for the British. Because of this, Jefferson said that ships from other countries could not take goods out of the United States. Ships stayed away and businesses across the United States lost money.

Jefferson went back to his home, Monticello, in 1809. Like George Washington, he said he would only serve two terms as president.

Monticello

*Monticello was not just a house. It was also a farm and a **plantation**. After his presidency, Jefferson had some money problems because Monticello was too expensive to run.*

One of Jefferson's dreams was for each American to get an education. In Jefferson's time, there were no public schools. Families had to send their children to private schools or pay **tutors.**

Jefferson and Adams

*Jefferson died on the same day that John Adams did—July 4, 1826. It was 50 years after both men had signed the **Declaration of Independence.***

Jefferson was able to talk the Virginia **legislature** into setting aside money for public education and for a state college. The college, the University of Virginia, became one of the finest in the United States. It is in Charlottesville, Virginia.

Jefferson designed the buildings at the college, including the one in the picture, the Rotunda. He also laid out the campus and picked the teachers.

Remembering Jefferson

Jefferson was one of the smartest presidents the United States ever had. He found many things in life interesting. Instead of keeping all of his knowledge to himself, he shared it with the people of the nation.

Jefferson was able to write words so well that when people read them they were proud to be Americans. His beautiful words in the **Declaration of Independence** helped Americans realize why they were fighting for their freedom.

The Jefferson Memorial in Washington, D.C., opened on April 13, Jefferson's birthday, in 1943.

Jefferson is one of four presidents shown on a sculpture on Mount Rushmore in South Dakota. He is right next to George Washington.

Jefferson dreamed of things that could be and tried his best to make those dreams come true. He dreamed of a country in which everyone would be equal to each other. He also thought that every person should have an equal say in how the nation was run. In many ways, Jefferson's dreams came true.

Jefferson helped shape the United States into what it is today—strong, independent, and free.

Glossary

boycott when a group of people refuse to buy, sell, or use any goods that another group produces

colony group of people who move to another land but are still ruled by the same country they moved away from. People who live in a colony are called colonists.

Continental Congress group of men that spoke and acted for the colonies that became the United States. It was formed to deal with complaints against Great Britain.

Declaration of Independence document that said the United States was an independent nation. Independent means not being under the control or rule of another person or government.

electoral vote vote in a presidential election from a person, an elector, who represents an area of the United States. This elector votes for the same person that most of the people he or she represents did in the general election.

governor person who is elected to lead a state

House of Representatives one of the bodies of the U.S. government that, along with the Senate, makes laws for the United States

legislature group of elected people who make, change, or get rid of laws

Parliament group of people who make the laws for Great Britain and its colonies

plantation large farm on which one main crop is grown by workers who live there

Revolutionary War war from 1775 to 1783 in which the American colonists won freedom from Great Britain. A revolution replaces one government by force with another government or ruling group.

term length of time an elected official serves. The term of office for the president is four years.

tutor teacher who teaches one student at a time

More Books to Read

Santella, Andrew. *Thomas Jefferson: Voice of Liberty.* Danbury, Conn.: Children's Press, 2000.

Welsbacher, Anne. *Thomas Jefferson.* Edina, Minn.: ABDO Publishing, 2000.

Places to Visit

Monticello

931 Thomas Jefferson Parkway

Charlottesville, Virginia 22902

Visitor Information: (434) 984-9800

Library of Congress

101 Independence Avenue SE

Washington, D.C. 20540

Visitor Information: (202) 707-9779

Index

Adams, John 20–23, 27

Blue Ridge Mountains 9

Bonaparte, Napoleon 24–25

books 7, 10–11

Boston Tea Party 15

Burr, Aaron 23

Charlottesville, Virginia 27

Clark, William 25

Continental Congress 16–17

Declaration of Independence 5, 6, 16–17, 27, 28

France 20–21, 24

Franklin, Ben 20

Great Britain 6, 14, 16–17, 18

Hamilton, Alexander 21, 22, 23

Houdon, Jean-Antoine 5

Italy 13

Jefferson, Jane 6, 10

Jefferson, Lucy 20

Jefferson, Martha 11, 20

Jefferson, Martha Wayles Skelton 11, 20

Jefferson, Peter 6–7

Lewis, Meriwether 25

Library of Congress 10

Louisiana Purchase 24–25

Louisiana Territory 24–25

Monticello 9, 10, 11, 26

Mount Rushmore 29

Parliament 14–15, 16

Philadelphia, Pennsylvania 16

Piedmont Valley 9

Revolutionary War 16

Rhode Island 4

rice 13

Sacagawea 25

Shadwell 6, 10

Spain 24

taxes 14–15, 16, 18

University of Virginia 27

Virginia 4, 6–9, 14, 16–20, 27

Washington, George 21–22, 26, 29

William and Mary, College of 7

Williamsburg, Virginia 7–8

Wythe, George 8